"With love and care, we can create a world where all creatures live in harmony, offering a bright and vibrant future for generations to come. Let's color together this dream of preservation and protection of animals!"

Jacqueline M Bueno

2024

This Book Belongs to:

____

Test Color Page

EAGLE

RHINO

MOUSE

SEA TURTLE

FROG

BUTTERFLY

MOOSE

PUPPY

SNAIL

SEAHORSE

HORSE

SWAN

OWL

SQUIRREL

ELEPHANT

STAR OF THE SEA

HEN

CAT

GIRAFFE

LION

LADYBIRD

BIRDIE

ORANGUTAN

FISH

DEFINITELY

WOODPECKER

HEDGEHOG

FOX

PORK

OCTOPUS

TIGER

SHARK

BEE

SNAKE

RABBIT

HIPOPPOTAMUS

ALLIGATOR

PENGUIN